Would you like to ride with. . .

Famous Texas

Ranchers

**Stories of ten famous ranchers
and places to visit to learn
more about them**

by Jane Alexander Knapik

EAKIN PRESS ★ Austin, Texas

To the memory of my ancestors,
Samuel and Thurzy Alexander,
who began ranching in Burnet County, Texas,
in the 1850s.

FIRST EDITION

Copyright © 1996
By Jane Alexander Knapik

Published in the United States of America
By Eakin Press
A Division of Sunbelt Media, Inc.
P. O. Drawer 90159 ★ Austin, Texas 78709-0159

2   3   4   5   6   7   8   9

ISBN 1-57168-107-8

Library of Congress Cataloging-in-Publication Data

Knapik, Jane.
    Would you like to ride with . . . famous Texas ranchers : stories of
ten famous ranchers — with places to visit to learn more about
them / by Jane Alexander Knapik. — 1st ed.
        p.   cm.
    Includes bibliographical references and index.
    Summary: Presents short biographies of ten noted Texas ranchers,
including Charles Schreiner, Watt Matthews, and Mary Nan West.
    ISBN 1-57168-107-8
    1. Ranchers—Texas—Biography—Juvenile literature. 2. Texas—
Biographical—Juvenile literature. 3. Ranch life—Texas—
Anecdotes—Juvenile literature. [1. Ranchers—Texas. 2. Texas—
Biography. 3. Ranch life—Texas.] I. Title.
F385.K68   1996
976.4'0099-dc20
[B]   96-24042
                                                        CIP
                                                        AC

Contents

Preface

Texans are proud of the ranching traditions of their state. The Texas ranchers presented in this book helped develop some of these traditions. They provided some colorful chapters in the state's history.

The first ranchers came to Texas more than 200 years ago. The ranchers represented here lived all across Texas, from Richmond to Brackettville, from Albany to Corpus Christi.

In this book, a young rancher first introduces you to the subject of ranching. Then, ten famous Texas ranchers are described. The lives of the ten were very different. For instance, Watt Matthews of Albany spent his entire life on one ranch. Rancher Dolph Briscoe became governor of Texas. Richard King was a riverboat pilot before he developed a new breed of cattle, the Santa Gertrudis.

But the ranchers were alike in several important ways. All of them had good business sense. Each helped develop the ranching industry and helped improve livestock. In spite of many problems, they were strong enough and smart enough to keep their property. And they all seemed to share a deep love for the ranching life. You'll see why.

U
Acknowledgments

Ranchers who helped with materials in the book were former Governor Dolph Briscoe, Mary Nan West, J.T. "Happy" Shahan, Donna Davis Schuster, and Frankie Henry Nelson, who is a Saunders descendant.

Other individuals who contributed were Michael Moore, executive director of the Fort Bend Museum Association; personnel at Lambshead Ranch; staff members of El Progreso Library in Uvalde; Wilson and Perna Reaves of Rosenberg; and friends Dr. Barbara Baethe, Margaret Davis, Edith Huddleston, Elizabeth Knippa, Donna Robinson, Mary Wallace, and Barbara Woodman.

The Ranching Life

As Lived by a Young Rancher

It is easy for me to understand why the ten Texas ranchers in this book wanted to become ranchers. I understand because I've always wanted to ranch.

My parents didn't push me into this work. It had to be my decision.

The toughest challenge for me, of course, is having enough money to start ranching. I can't afford to buy a whole ranch, full of livestock. The best way for me to start was by leasing my own 4,600-acre place. That was just before I finished college at Texas A&M.

My older sister Dana and I owned Angora goats together for several years. When I was ready to stock my place, I started with about 1,400 goats. Then I added 100 Charbray heifers, branded with my Standing Two brand.

Goats and cattle are a good combination for my ranch. On one side of the place, there is brush for the goats to browse. The other side has the river and good cow pasture.

Of course, my parents Dan and Margaret Davis have had a big influence on me. I grew up on a ranch. Dana and I helped with all the work that went on at home. That means everything. We helped Mom prepare meals. We tended to sick animals and rode horseback to herd livestock if Dad needed us.

I started riding my horse, Bay Dollie, when I was three. That was my first year to enter Youth Rodeo barrel racing. I learned the racing patterns by running them on foot in the living room.

Bay Dollie had already been trained to follow those patterns around the barrels set up in the rodeo arena. She had learned the patterns years before I was even born.

When I was in school, the Youth Rodeo Association and the 4-H Club were my favorite organizations. In 4-H activities, I gained self-confidence. I learned to talk in front of a group or to ask questions when necessary. In the cooking events, I was best at making snacks, desserts, and breads. Everything a person does in 4-H has to be written into a record book. My record book in foods and nutrition won me a trip to Chicago for the National 4-H Congress.

The saddle my parents bought me for Youth Rodeo barrel racing is the one I still use every day. The saddle is lightweight and easy for me to carry and put on my horse. I added toe fenders to protect my boots because I ride through so much brush.

When I'm working, I don't look too much like the usual rancher you might see on television. I wear jeans, a short-sleeved shirt, Red Wing work shoes, and a baseball cap. For work in the brush, I change to long sleeves and add leggings.

I spend a lot of time in my pickup truck. But for horseback riding, Esperanza, a thirteen-year-old bay mare, is the only horse I've used in recent years.

When I ride her to round up goats at shearing time, she knows just what to do. She really watches every goat. If a goat stops, she stops. If a goat turns out of the bunch, she quickly goes to get it back.

A rancher always can tell you what kind of work will be going on months ahead of time. Early in the year, I gather, drench, and shear the goats. By March, the goat kids and the calves are born. Shots have to be given to prevent diseases among the animals. Then it is time to ear-mark the goat kids and to dehorn the calves and castrate, or neuter, the bull calves.

August brings shearing time again for goats. Kids are weaned and separated from the nannies in September. Calves are weaned in October. I cull out some animals and sell them. Others are kept for the herds.

Out on my place, I always watch for any signs of coyotes, bobcats, hawks, or wild hogs. If they kill any livestock, I contact a government trapper. He will trap the predators or give me permission to shoot them.

Of course, I have to sell livestock at the right time to make a profit. Another way to make a profit from my ranch is to lease it out to hunters. They hunt for deer, turkey, and wild hogs.

In the future, I will have better quality cattle and goats. Also, I will work to control mesquite brush and keep fences in good conditions.

My husband, John Paul, an agricultural science teacher, understands everything that happens on the ranch. On his days off, he always helps me.

In ranching, I never get caught up with my work. Getting up early, at 5:00 A.M., is a must. Even when I don't work livestock, I have other chores such as mending fences and cleaning water troughs. Something new happens every day on the ranch. That's why I like ranching.

The famous Texas ranchers in this book took risks like I'm taking now. I expect to give the ranching business my very best effort. I also plan to enjoy every minute of the work.

Donna Davis Schuster
Brackettville, Texas

Famous Texas Ranchers of the 20th Century

James T. "Happy" Shahan,
in front of his Alamo Village in Brackettville.
— Courtesy Virginia Shahan

Happy Shahan

The "Singing Rancher"

*WOULD YOU like to ride a horse in a movie
or on a television show?
Happy Shahan could show you how.*

James T. "Happy" Shahan of Brackettville brought
Hollywood to Texas. Part of his 17,000-acre ranch
became a location for Hollywood movie productions.
But his main work was ranching. Most of the ranch
land was used to raise fine livestock, including Longhorn cattle, which carry the HV brand.

When he was young, Happy had never thought
about being a rancher. All he wanted to do was study
sociology and play basketball at Baylor University.
His Baylor teammates gave him the nickname
"Happy." They noticed that he usually "laughed his
way through problems."

At Baylor, Happy married Virginia Webb. Her
father was a rancher near Brackettville. The ranch
was important to Virginia. Happy didn't know anything about ranching, but he knew he could learn.

"I had to learn almost everything," Happy said. "For instance, I learned how to work on windmills. I knew how to ride a horse, but I didn't know how to shoe a horse. I heard there was a horseshoeing class at Fort Clark, a cavalry post near the ranch. The soldiers taught me the way it should be done."

Soon after they moved to the ranch, Virginia promised Happy a special gift. It was his first pair of Western boots. They went to San Antonio to have the boots made at the famous Lucchese boot shop.

One of the first things they had to do on their ranch was to select a cattle brand. The HV brand stands for the owners' names, Happy and Virginia.

 They used the brand on their first herd of Angus cattle and on all their livestock after that.

On the ranch, the Shahans raised their three children, Jamie, Tulisha and Tully. Happy liked to tell stories about the children's years on the ranch. When their son Tully was four years old, he had a horse named "Goldbrick." On a ride alone out in the pasture, Tully often liked to get off his horse for a few minutes. He wanted to look for interesting rocks. When the boy was ready to remount, he would touch Goldbrick's leg a certain way. The horse would kneel down so Tully could get back on the saddle.

"There were ranch problems I didn't expect," Happy said. "For instance, during World War II, I had some problems with Fort Clark. The military needed to use 8,000 acres on the south end of the ranch just for practice.

"One day, I found out that some soldiers had been cutting the fences. They crossed into areas where they had no business. They used our buildings for target practice. That shooting disturbed ranch hands who lived nearby. After I proved to the fort commander that it had happened, he made sure the shooting stopped."

Happy thought of many ways to make money on the ranch. Along with ranch work the first winter, he trapped raccoons, ringtails, bobcats, and fox. Somebody bought the pelts for $20 to $40 each. Another time he built a thirty-mile track on the ranch for off-road racing.

He decided to learn to rope and win fees at calf-roping contests. He set up a roping ring to practice on the ranch. Later he won four calf-roping contests. The roping horse was named "Texas," his favorite horse of all time.

The Shahans also opened several businesses in nearby Brackettville. Their customers were the town's population of 4,800 people, including the military families at Fort Clark.

Then, in 1944, Brackettville had a problem. The army closed Fort Clark, and many people moved away. With the smaller population, all Brackettville businesses had a hard time. Two years later, a Houston company bought old Fort Clark from the government and opened a guest ranch. That gave some help to businesses in town, but they needed more jobs for the people who lived there.

Happy and other town leaders started having meetings. They talked about what they could do to bring jobs to town. They didn't have enough money to bring in big business.

At one meeting, Happy had an unusual idea. He said, "We ought to try to make movies here!"

People said he was crazy. They said nobody from Hollywood would come to Brackettville to make movies. When he went home and told Virginia about the idea, even she said, "You're crazy!"

Anyway, Happy went to Hollywood to ask producers to consider Brackettville. He always liked to promote things. He carried an album with photos of his town to show to anybody who would listen. For nine days, no one listened.

Happy didn't give up. On the tenth day, he talked with an important man at Paramount Studio. After Happy talked a long time, the man finally agreed to film the movie *Arrowhead* at Fort Clark. It was the first picture made in the Brackettville area.

In 1955, *Last Command* was filmed at another location near the little town. Then Happy overheard someone from Hollywood say that John Wayne was going to make a movie to be called *The Alamo*.

"I called Wayne and asked if I could come out to California to see him," Happy said. "We had a disagreement over the phone. He said he was going to do the movie in Mexico. I said, 'You can't make it in Mexico. You have to make it in Texas.'

"I spent a lot of time arguing with Wayne by phone. In fact, we argued for two and a half years. Then, I went out to California for eight days. I spent part of every day with John Wayne. We just argued more, but these were friendly arguments. Finally, he agreed to send a man down to see our ranch."

4

Things turned out the way Happy had hoped. He built the first permanent movie set in Texas right there on the Shahan ranch. It was built for John Wayne's epic movie *The Alamo.*

Construction on the set started in September 1957 and took almost two years to complete. Happy wanted the set to look like San Antonio in the early 1800s, just before the Battle of the Alamo.

Workers used more than a million adobe bricks, twelve miles of water pipe, and 30,000 square feet of imported Spanish roofing tile. They then added a huge amount of concrete flooring to complete the Village.

The set later was opened to visitors. It became known as Happy Shahan's Alamo Village. Everyone especially liked the full-size copy of the most famous Texas shrine, the Alamo. The set also included a cemetery, town jail, bank, various frontier shops, the Old San Fernando Church, a museum, and a prize herd of registered Texas Longhorn cattle.

One friendly argument between John Wayne and Happy concerned those Longhorns. "He told me he wanted Longhorn steers," Happy said. "We didn't have any on the ranch. I had to go out and buy twenty steers and start training them for the movie."

Filming for *The Alamo* began in August 1959. The cost was over $12 million. It was the largest amount spent on making a film in the United States at that time.

Alamo Village later served as the set for more than sixty films besides *The Alamo.* Other productions were the IMAX film *Alamo: The Price of Freedom*, television shows including *Lonesome Dove* and *Texas*, and many commercials. The set was stocked with stagecoaches, wagons, buggies, surreys, and guns. It had everything a Western story might need.

Happy himself became known as the "Singing Rancher" when he recorded in Nashville. He often had bit parts in movies made at the ranch. "Cowboy," a sorrel with four stocking legs and a white streak on his face, was the horse he rode in movies.

With the movie sets in place, the Shahan ranch was worth more. But ranching was always the main business for the Shahans.

Ranch soil around Brackettville is shallow, with lots of big rocks. The worst problem a rancher could have in that country is drought. Happy had to raise animals that could survive on that dry land. He found that crossbred cattle, Angora and Spanish goats, Ramboillet and Suffolk sheep did well enough.

Of course, the hardiest animals were the Longhorn cattle. While buying Longhorns for John Wayne, Happy started his own herd. He made more money with his Longhorns than from other cattle.

Hunters were another source of income for the ranch. Wild game that brought hunters was mainly turkey and deer. Happy also found that people would buy native plants, everything from prickly pear cactus to trees. They especially liked the evergreen mountain laurel for decorations.

On the ranch, Happy spent some of his time overseeing ranch hands working with livestock. He often rode his favorite work horse, a sorrel named "Star."

Other times he worked at his home office or welcomed visitors to the Village. He dressed in

Western wear, with Lucchese boots and a wide choice of Western hats.

Happy could always think of lots of things to do right there on the ranch. In 1994, for instance, he decided to stage a Texas Longhorn Quincentennial Celebration at Alamo Village. It marked the 500th anniversary of the coming of the first Texas Longhorns to Texas. Christopher Columbus brought them to the Americas in 1494.

The Village on Happy's ranch also served as a training ground for young actors and singers. They practiced their talents during summer shows at the Village. Sometimes they acted in movies made at the ranch.

When Happy died in 1996, he was buried on his beloved ranch. Just as he had wished, the Shahan family and the Alamo Village "family" were the only ones present for the funeral service. The casket was made in the Village workshop by cowboys, who carved an HV on it. A cowboy procession included a horse with the traditional empty saddle. A son-in-law conducted the funeral service, which was followed by a rifle salute fired by Village cowboys.

Happy Shahan became a famous Texas rancher after he found out how to attract Hollywood to Texas. Though Happy is gone, his memory is very much alive. The Village is still open to the public.

Dolph Briscoe, Jr., former governor of Texas.
— Courtesy Dolph Briscoe, Jr.

Dolph Briscoe, Jr.

A Texas Rancher Who Served as Governor

WOULD YOU like to be governor of Texas?
Rancher Dolph Briscoe did that.

Most Texans know the name of Dolph Briscoe, Jr., a Uvalde rancher. He served as the governor of Texas from 1973 to 1979.

He also is well known because he is the largest individual landowner in Texas.

Dolph Briscoe, Jr., was born in Uvalde, west of San Antonio, on April 23, 1923. As a youngster, he always knew ranching was for him. His father, Dolph Briscoe, Sr., owned large ranches in the Rio Grande brush country. Dolph, Jr., wanted to be just like his father.

"During the summers when I was very young, the work I liked was riding," he said. "Pinto was the name of the Shetland paint that I learned to ride on. I liked riding better than working on fences or the windmill. We rode most days, usually looking for calves that were sick because of screwworms."

Dolph explained why he used the Open Six brand. His father was a partner with Ross Sterling, who later became governor of Texas. The livestock they owned together always carried the Open Nine brand.

"In the 1930s, my father de-veloped the Open Six brand. It's an easy brand. I've always used it as my brand, also. The same branding iron can be turned upside down for the Open Nine brand that we use for partnership cattle."

When Dolph was in high school, his father gave him a saddle made in Uvalde by Will Slade. It always was his favorite saddle. His hat always was gray felt. He kept hats for a very long time, thirty years or more.

In high school he also had two pairs of Lucchese boots from San Antonio. The boots had medium heels and were high boots, almost to the knee. One pair had Dolph's initials in the design. The other pair carried the Open Six brand.

The Briscoes bought many ranches through the years. Hacienda Las Margaritas, a 225,000-acre ranch in Mexico, was the one Dolph liked best. He had the chance to spend time there when school was out for the summer. It was his idea that he would stay there after he graduated from Uvalde High School in 1939. His father had a different idea, however. The senior Briscoe hoped that his son would get a law degree at the University of Texas in Austin.

Dolph graduated from the university in 1942. He married Janey Slaughter of Austin. Then he went into the United States Army during World War II. There never was time for law school.

After the war, Dolph still wanted to be a rancher. When Janey and Dolph moved to Uvalde in 1946, his father turned over the sheep and goat business to them. The young couple lived on the Dry Frio River ranch and also leased other rangeland. They had about 20,000 acres for sheep and goats, along with a few cattle.

Their children, Janey, Chip and Cele, learned to ride on a Shetland named Star. Then a friend gave them an older horse named Braniff. He had some racing background, but he was very gentle and fine for them.

"We had good years," Dolph said. "Then I wanted to do something in addition to ranching. That's why I ran for the Texas Legislature."

He would serve four terms in Austin as a Texas representative, from 1949 to 1957.

One hot issue in 1949 was how to get farmers and ranchers "out of the mud." Country roads were a problem in bad weather. Dolph helped write the 1949 legislative bill to build Farm-to-Market roads in Texas. Farmers and ranchers then had the best system of rural roads of any state. He also helped get telephones to country families in 1951.

Dolph didn't run for the legislative seat again after his father's death in 1954. Instead, he and his family stayed in Uvalde to run the entire Briscoe ranching business. On the Catarina Ranch, Dolph increased the number of Santa Gertrudis cattle. The Briscoe herd of Santa Gertrudis came from the famous King Ranch in South Texas.

In 1960, Dolph was elected president of an important organization, the Texas and Southwestern Cattle Raisers Association. He and other members wanted to find out how to kill all the screwworms in Texas. They knew how many head of livestock died every year because of the insects.

A blowfly lays eggs on any wound or cut that an animal might have. The eggs turn into larvae that ranchers call "screwworms."

When the screwworm problem was so bad, Texas ranchers worked livestock every day, looking for sick animals. They would "doctor" the animals that had screwworms. Then those sick animals were placed in a pen called the "worm trap" and doctored again. This work went on at least six days in every week. Still the worms would kill young calves, sheep, and goats.

"We ranchers were desperate," Dolph remembered. "We had to do something."

Not many people thought the screwworm problem could be stopped. Then the news came that scientists in Florida had learned how to kill blowflies.

"Their work cost lots of money," Dolph said. "We organized the Southwest Animal Health Research Foundation. Ranchers raised over $3 million to get the scientists started in Texas. Hunters also gave money. They knew that screwworms killed many deer fawns born every year."

Lyndon Johnson was president of the United States then. He was a Texas rancher who knew about the screwworm problem. He agreed to get other important people to listen to Dolph's group. Help came from the Department of Agriculture and from officials in Mexico. The U.S. Senate also gave $100,000 for research.

Finally, the program began to work. Animals no longer died because of screwworms. Dolph had kept at the problem until a solution was found. The Junior Chamber of Commerce named him "Outstanding Young Texan" for his efforts.

Now the program is used as far south as Panama. All ranchers keep careful watch, however. If anyone in Texas sees signs of screwworms, he calls a county official for help.

Dolph Briscoe, Jr., returned to Austin as governor of Texas from 1973 to 1979. While serving all the people of Texas, he especially understood the needs of farmers and ranchers.

Dolph Briscoe wanted to see young Texans more active in politics and legislation. "Our democracy is not going to work unless we participate," he said. "Everyone needs to participate in his or her own way. Some can help by holding some sort of public office. Certainly, everyone can participate by voting."

He also encouraged young people to become ranchers. Dolph believed that the future was bright for cattle raisers. "I think people can eat beef every day of the week and not get tired of it," he said.

Dolph's son, Chip, always wanted to be a rancher. When Chip finished college, he chose to ranch near Cotulla. "Ranching has changed a lot in my lifetime," Dolph said. "We used to do our ranch work with horses. Now my son uses a helicopter for rounding up his livestock. Even with new technology, though, ranching still requires a tremendous amount of work."

Dolph inherited 190,000 acres of land from his parents. In his lifetime, he added 230,000 acres. As board chairman of Briscoe Ranch, Inc., he managed land, cattle, oil and gas interests on Briscoe property.

Dolph Briscoe received many honors. For instance, the University of Texas Health Science Center at San Antonio opened the Dolph Briscoe Library. Texas A&M University gave him the Distinguished Texan in Agriculture Award.

"I wanted to be a rancher from the very beginning," Dolph stated again. "However, I wouldn't take anything for having served as governor of Texas."

Texans will remember Dolph Briscoe as one of their governors. But they won't forget that he was a rancher, first and foremost.

Mary Nan West

Hall of Fame Rancher

*WOULD YOU like to ride a palomino horse in
a stock show parade?*
Mary Nan West did that.

Mary Nan West owns the 36,000-acre Rafter S
Ranch 100 miles southwest of San Antonio. That
ranch in the brush country of Zavala County used to
belong to her grandparents. It was always special to
Mary Nan because she grew up there.

Mary Nan's grandfather,
George Washington West, established the Rafter S Ranch in
1903, more than twenty years
before Mary Nan was born.

In her childhood, Mary Nan
learned important lessons from
both grandparents. Her grand-

mother, Robbie West, wanted Mary Nan to be a lady.
Her grandfather said a woman could do anything a
man could and still be a lady doing it.

Mary Nan West of the Rafter S, Batesville.
— Courtesy Mary Nan West

Grandfather West also gave Mary Nan certain values to guide her. "Never tell a lie," he taught her. "Never choose friends based on their color, religion or wealth." He also gave Mary Nan the nickname "Pet," a name her friends would use all her life.

Grandfather West was happy to have his granddaughter turn out to be a "tomboy." She could shoot a gun when she was four. Soon afterward, she started working cattle.

Mary Nan first attended school in the nearby community of Batesville. Like other ranch youngsters then, she studied at home by a kerosene lamp. Rural families didn't have electricity until years later.

Mary Nan finished the sixth grade in Batesville. Then her grandparents enrolled her at St. Mary's Hall, a girls' school in San Antonio. Her grandfather explained why he was sending her there. "I want you to learn to be as much at home in someone's parlor as you are on a horse," he said.

Mary Nan lived at the school except for vacations. She missed the freedom of living on a ranch. She missed her family, and she missed her favorite animals. (Even today, she has a number of pets. They range from dogs and cats to a twenty-year-old Hereford named Gertrude. That Hereford began life as an orphan calf, bottle-fed by Mary Nan.)

After St. Mary's, Mary Nan could not attend Texas A&M. Girls could not enroll at the college then. Instead, she attended college in California and other western states. She always wanted to take useful courses, such as auto mechanics.

Then, at age eighteen, she returned to the ranch. It was the only place she ever really wanted to be. By that time, the 1940s, her grandparents had grown old and needed her to be near. They wanted her to manage the ranch and its Hereford cattle operation.

On the ranch, she knew how to work right along with the cowboys. She could take care of roping, inoculating or branding cattle.

In later years, Mary Nan's two daughters also grew up on the Rafter S Ranch. They worked alongside their mother just as she had worked with her grandfather.

"My sister Robbie and I had jobs we were assigned," said Mary West Traylor. "We worked our baby calves during the winter. My job was to do the cooking and the branding. Robbie rode horseback, gathered cattle, and helped in the pens."

In the 1960s, when her daughters were grown, Mary Nan volunteered to help at the San Antonio Livestock Exposition, Inc. She enjoyed working with her friend, Harry Freeman, who had started the stock show.

Mary Nan knew how to get other people to work with her. A volunteer corps of 2,400 men and women agreed to help. Mary Nan welcomed anybody who wanted to work on behalf of youth. The volunteers were happy to know that most of the stock show profits went to youth programs.

The San Antonio stock show became an important event for Mary Nan. She took along her two Missouri Fox Trotter palomino horses from the ranch. Yellow Rose was the one that carried the American flag during the grand entry. Goldie was the horse that Mary Nan rode.

By 1984, Mary Nan helped the stock show to set

up a college scholarship fund. The money went to students studying agriculture and science at Texas colleges. Within ten years, the San Antonio stock show had awarded more than $5.2 million in scholarships.

The San Antonio show also started another program to give San Antonio schoolchildren information about the food chain. Mary Nan wanted youngsters who lived in town to know who raised the food they ate.

On the Rafter S Ranch, Mary Nan always found time to manage her ranch business. She made sure that her ranch kept up with changes, like using pickups instead of horses. In the 1960s she also constructed her own ranch home. It was a good place for entertaining guests. They came from far and near to visit this Texas rancher.

She relied on help from her grandson, George West Bodden. He became foreman of the Rafter S Ranch. Part of his training came from his classes at A&M. The rest he learned from his grandmother and her ranch staff.

"My grandmother taught me some good rules," he said. "She said that before you can tell anybody what to do, you have to know how to do it yourself."

In 1991, Texas Governor Ann Richards appointed Mary Nan to the board of regents of the Texas A&M University System. Later she was the first woman to be elected chairman of that board. She believed the board gave her an important opportunity again to serve young Texans.

Mary Nan sometimes reminded people that the "A" in "A&M" stands for agriculture. She believed that agriculture is the root of the entire school. She knew that research programs at A&M gave important information to farmers and ranchers.

Mary Nan spent more than half her time on the A&M work. Sometimes, she went to the campus. Other times, she worked in her office at the ranch. It took lots of her time to read all the A&M board materials.

On the College Station campus, Brooke Leslie was the first girl to be elected student body president at A&M. While in high school, Brooke had won a San Antonio stock show scholarship. That was when she met Mary Nan. Later, Brooke presided at student senate meetings that Mary Nan attended on the A&M campus.

Mary Nan West's work in agriculture helped many young Texans. For her service to others, she was honored as a member of the Texas Women's Hall of Fame. Her name also is found in the Heritage Hall of Honor at the State Fair in Dallas.

Watt Matthews

The Princeton Graduate

WOULD YOU rather work on a ranch than go to school?
  Watt Matthews tried that one year.

Watkins Reynolds Matthews lived near Albany, west of Fort Worth. His nickname was "Watt." He ran the 40,000-acre Lambshead Ranch that he and his sisters inherited from their parents. It was named for Lambshead Creek that ran through the ranch.

Watt lived a long life, almost 100 years, on the ranch that he loved. He was born there on February 1, 1899.

He never wanted to do anything but work on the ranch. However, his mother, Sallie Matthews, had other ideas for Watt, her youngest child. She was the teacher for her children on the ranch. She wanted Watt to study hard at home so he could go to college.

When Watt was ten years old, however, he es-

Watkins Reynolds Matthews
— Drawing by Paul Cameron Smith

caped school one year. His father, J.A. Matthews, needed him to help with ranch work.

"No one believed in hard work more than our father," Watt said.

As it turned out, Watt had to make up the lost school time the following year. He spent long hours at a desk in the main house. He learned geography, history, reading, spelling, arithmetic, and penmanship. His older sisters helped their mother check on his progress.

"Mamma didn't want me to be a cattleman," Watt said. "She thought we already had plenty of cow people in the family. That's why she sent me to college."

After graduating from Princeton University, Watt returned to Lambshead. He stayed and became ranch manager.

"I just couldn't leave," he said of his ranch home. He took trips away from Texas, even out of the United States. But he mainly liked to stay at home or go visiting at a nearby ranch.

Watt took good care of the land and the livestock. He was careful about how he invested ranch money. The family was happy when oil and gas wells were drilled on Lambshead to add to the family income.

Lambshead ran Hereford cattle, a breed of red and white cattle with horns. Watt liked them because they seemed to survive droughts better than other cattle.

Lambshead cow ponies came from a small herd of brood mares. The ranch stallion was a quarter horse named Go Dog Go. The horses were small and tough, stout enough to carry a cowboy all day in rough country.

In his work at Lambshead, Watt added technology to help with ranch work. He thought a helicopter pilot could be considered a modern cowboy. At roundup time, the pilot helped find cattle. The noise of his helicopter scared the cattle out of the underbrush. Then cowboys on horseback could herd them more easily.

During roundups and branding, ranchers got together to help each other. Every person had a certain job to do. For more than seventy years, Watt was the man who did the branding. All Lambshead cattle were branded to prove ownership.

The AV brand Watt used was registered by his father in 1885. The "Open A" along with the "Lazy V" of Watt's brand made a simple, clear outline on an animal's side.

Besides Hereford cattle, Watt kept his own herd of Longhorns. He used a different brand for them. It was the Spanish Gourd, the brand his grandfather used. Longhorns are larger than Herefords. A Longhorn steer can grow six feet high at the shoulders and weigh over 2,000 pounds. It has a brindled hide and always looks wild.

Watt also had a herd of buffalo, just for historic reasons. Buffalo were on the land in earliest times. They roamed at will across Lambshead just as they did when Indians lived in Texas. The huge animals often tore down fences that got in their way. Cowboys on horseback had trouble trying to herd them.

Conservation of grassland was important to

Watt. He was careful not to let cattle overgraze a pasture. Ranch hands cut out mesquite brush and prickly pear so that grass could grow better. The ranch needed good grass for livestock and for wildlife like quail, turkey, and deer.

Visitors to Lambshead sometimes thought they had taken a step back in time to the days of the Old West. That was because Watt restored old buildings that are part of ranch history.

One old building was a stone "dugout." Early settlers used it as a home. The back wall of the dugout actually was the side of a hill. Thick stone walls formed the other three sides.

Ranch headquarters included several old homes. Watt moved them to Lambshead from other historic ranches. The bed in which Watt was born was displayed in one of these houses.

He also preserved the Reynolds house, where his parents were married in 1876. Then there was the Stone Ranch house, where his mother lived as a child. Watt also added to his collection a copy of an old, one-room schoolhouse.

Headquarters buildings on Lambshead Ranch were painted red. Houses were trimmed in white and arranged under pecan trees and red oaks. One house was large enough for all the Matthews family and their friends to gather. Smaller houses belonged to Watt's sisters.

Watt's bedroom was located in the red bunkhouse. It was a simple room, just the way he liked it, with a narrow bed, a chest of drawers, a chair, and a boot jack.

For Watt, the ranch was the very center of his

life. On a typical work day, he was up at 5:15 A.M. His everyday clothes were a Western shirt with buttons (not snaps) a pair of Levis, boots, and denim jacket. He wore high-heeled boots like all cowboys used to wear. Tan boots were his choice for ranch work, and black ones were for church or other special events.

The rancher's hat was soft felt so that the brim would "give" if he rode through brush. Before wearing the hat for the first time, Watt held it over a steaming kettle in the "cookshack." The steam helped him mold the hat into his favorite style with a crown that was not too high. Watt's best Stetson hat had a gray and black horsehair band that was woven years ago by his mother.

After Watt dressed, he went to the cookshack. It was a building for cooking and dining. The cook served breakfast for the family and for ranch hands at 5:45 A.M. The two fireplaces burned mesquite wood on cool mornings and added the smell of smoke to the area.

Watt also used the cookshack for his business office. Every day, he spent time at his desk. In a small book, he wrote about work done on the ranch. He also described the weather, even the amount of rainfall and the direction of the wind. Weather is always important to ranchers.

Sometimes Watt used his cookshack office for meetings with cattle buyers or other business people. When his office work was done, Watt usually took a drive in his pickup. He liked to oversee work done by ranch hands.

At Lambshead Ranch, everyone took time off for the noon meal called "dinner." Watt's dinner guests usually arrived in pickups. They sometimes included oil field workers, a scientist from the university, a helicopter pilot, and other friends. Watt spoke English or Spanish with his visitors. Everyone went through the serving line to help himself to the ranch food. Watt's favorite food was black-eyed peas with *jalapeño* peppers. After the meal, everyone went back to work.

Those who knew Watt admired his character, his honesty, friendliness, and hard work. His friends enjoyed his company because he never complained or boasted.

Watt also was a generous man. His parents taught him to care about others. He and his family supported activities in Albany, the town near the ranch.

Every year in June, citizens of Albany present "The Fandangle," a musical show. Watt got involved in the festivities. He often lent covered wagons and Longhorn cattle for the day. Before the main event, he invited the cast to stage a mini-Fandangle on his ranch.

Because of his work as a rancher, Watt received many awards. An outstanding award was the Golden Spur Award. It came from the Ranching Heritage Association of Texas Tech University in Lubbock.

No doubt about it — Watt Matthews served as a great example of ranching heritage in Texas.

Famous Texas Ranchers
of Earlier Years

Juan Flores

Spanish Rancher in Texas

WOULD YOU like to round up and brand your own herd of wild Longhorns?
Juan Flores could show you how.

Juan Jose Flores de Abrego y Valdes was a Spanish rancher. He was the first rancher to have a cattle brand issued to him in Texas. The old brands are much more ornate than the simple brands we see in Texas today.

Texas belonged to Spain when Juan registered his brand in 1762. He branded his livestock to show that they belonged to him. He used a hot branding iron to make a permanent mark on an animal's hide.

The brand was recorded in a book in old San Antonio. Now these books are the Bexar Archives. These old documents help us understand what life was like for Spanish-Texans.

At first, missionaries raised all the livestock in Texas. Later, the Spanish government gave land to men like Juan and allowed them to own livestock.

Juan came from his parents' home in Saltillo, Mexico, to ranch in Texas. He settled near the present town of Floresville.

Not far away from Juan lived his brother, Francisco Flores. Their neighbors also were important in the history of Texas ranchers. Andres Hernandez was the first person to own a ranch in Texas. Another neighbor was Luis Antonio Menchaca. He owned the largest Texas ranch at that time — 50,000 acres.

To get land, Juan promised to live on his ranch. The Spanish government also expected Juan to keep horses and guns ready for use. He might be ordered to fight Indians. They often made raids on the missions and the ranches. Not one place in all of Texas was safe from hostile Indians.

Juan and his wife, Dona Leonor Delgado, had four sons. Their names were Joachin, Pedro, Juan, Jr., and Jose Francisco. Two slaves also lived in their household.

Their first ranch home probably was a *jacal*, a small hut made from trees. The only fences they built were *corrals*, large enough to pen a few cattle, horses, mules, sheep, or goats near home.

Later, Juan built a sturdier home, partly underground. The house made of sandstone and adobe bricks wouldn't catch fire easily. Instead of windows, the houses had gun slits or small openings in the walls. The owner could climb on the flat roof of such a house and fight Indians from behind its roof railings.

In 1769, Lipans and Comanches made many raids on the ranchers in the San Antonio River Valley. Juan and the others helped the Spanish soldiers, but they lost most of the valley livestock. Only a few cattle hiding in the woods were left for the ranchers.

After several months of Indian battles, the ranchers were having a hard time. The problem was they couldn't fight Indians and still have time to take care of ranch work.

As a leader of the ranchers, Juan spoke up. He asked the Spanish governor to build a fort where ranch families could go for safety. Most of all, however, he wanted the families to be safe on their own ranches. He convinced the governor to assign twenty soldiers to guard the ranches.

When the Indians were not bothering his ranch workers, Juan rebuilt his herds from wild stock. New Spanish expeditions brought more and more livestock to Texas every year. Many unbranded animals broke away and became wild.

Juan could take his choice of Longhorn cattle  that had developed from Spanish cattle. Then he could select from among the wild Spanish horses. The horses were strong but small, usually only about thirteen hands high. They were of different colors.

Juan's workers rounded up the wild animals and drove them into fields near the houses. Then they tried to tame them. The men who worked with the livestock for Juan and other early ranchers were *vaqueros*, the first Texas cowboys.

These men were excellent horsemen. A rope, or *lasso*, was their favorite tool for working cattle. They brought to Texas the practice of "cow hunts" or cattle roundups.

Vaqueros needed clothes to protect them from Texas weather and heavy brush. The men wore wide-brimmed hats for protection from the sun. They had sturdy shirts, jackets, and pants. Often they wore buckskin leggings and stockings made of animal skins. Most *vaqueros* also wore a pair of enormous spurs on their heels to make their horses follow commands.

The saddles that Spaniards brought to Texas were uncomfortable for riding. Also, it was hard for a rider to dismount from those saddles. The Spanish-Texans spent lots of time on horseback, so they gradually changed the design of saddles. Then a horseman could ride more comfortably and safely. He could get on and off his horse quickly.

While men worked with livestock, Juan's wife, Dona Leonor, stayed busy at home. She brought fine home furnishings from Mexico. She supervised the other ranch wives in their work as homemakers. The women looked after the children and made family clothing. They also cleaned the houses, prepared meals, and tended the gardens. They were responsible for smaller ranch animals like chickens.

Dona Leonor knew how to take care of sick people. Also, she educated her children at home or sent them to school at the mission.

Juan and his sons learned about laws that affected their ranch. They knew how to defend themselves against unfair laws.

For religious services, the Flores family had an altar in their home. Dona Leonor arranged for baptisms, weddings, or funerals when a priest visited the ranch.

Sometimes they went to mass at the mission Espiritu Santo. It was located near Presidio La Bahia (the present town of Goliad). At the church, Spanish missionaries were busy with teaching and caring for Indians who lived at the mission. Indian students did not have books to study. Instead, the missionaries made up religious plays. They acted the plays out to teach religious stories to the Indians.

After religious services, the Flores family spent time in the *presidio*. They bought and traded for goods that other Spanish citizens brought to sell in the market. Some of them traded or sold horses and mules.

The Floreses visited with friends and relatives who had gathered for market days. While he visited with others, Juan always listened for news about Indian raids or new laws passed by Spanish officials.

Each year, Juan and his neighbors went on important trading trips to Saltillo, Mexico. They didn't drive livestock to market. Instead, they took pack mules loaded with animal hides, dried meat, fat, suet, and other animal products. They traded for blankets, cloth, flour, soap, pots, salt, candy, and chocolate before returning to Texas.

Indians were only one problem that ranchers had. Juan and his neighbors also had trouble with Spanish government officials. Ranchers didn't like paying Spanish taxes. And they really didn't like the laws about ownership of unbranded, stray animals.

Without fences, cattle and other livestock were allowed to run free in Texas. That meant that people would argue about ownership of the stock.

Juan had a reason for registering his own brand and for branding his livestock. He hoped that other stock owners would do the same. That way, they wouldn't argue over ownership.

There was a problem about who owned unbranded stock. Each rancher claimed all unbranded stock found near his property. This stock included young animals that had been born after branding time the year before.

Juan tried to explain to government officials why these strays belonged to him, even though they weren't branded. "Our cattle are scattered because of Indian raids and drought," he said. "These are our cattle. We have the right to gather them wherever we find them."

The missionaries disagreed with the ranchers. The church officials said the missions needed all stray livestock.

The Spanish governor took the side of the missionaries in the argument. He announced that all unbranded stock belonged to the missions. When he said that, the ranchers were very upset. It was a bitter experience for the ranchers to see their cattle taken away to the missions.

Juan thought the governor was wrong. He decided to ignore the law. He kept on branding the stray cattle that he found near his land.

Because Juan chose to break the law, the governor had him arrested. By that time, however, Juan was sixty-four years old and in poor health. The officials decided to keep him under "house arrest" at his home instead of in prison.

They expected Juan to obey their law. Again he chose to break the governor's law. He left his home and went with his brother Francisco. They drove a herd of 650 cattle to market in Monclova, Mexico.

Spanish-Texans were happier when a new governor was appointed. He tried to treat everyone fairly, including Juan. The first thing the governor did was to require ranchers and missions to brand their cattle every year. Also, ranchers had to register their brands with the governor. The new laws made it possible for ranchers to make a profit on their land again.

Juan died about 1779. He left a will to give his sons items that were important to Spanish-Texas ranchers. To his son Joachin, he left a mule and two tame horses. Pedro received a pair of oxen and two cows. For Juan, Jr., there were a tame mule and a horse. Jose Francisco was given his father's gun, sword, saddle, and a bridle with silver ornaments.

He also left great responsibilities for his sons. He and other Spanish-Texas ranchers had worked hard to start the ranching business in Texas. They wanted their sons to carry on, to protect themselves against Indians and against unfair government.

Now, more than 200 years after Juan lived in Texas, many Texans may claim him as an ancestor. The town of Floresville was named in honor of descendants of his rancher brother, Francisco Flores.

Texans honor Juan Flores de Abrego y Valdes as one of the first Texas ranchers. His brand is the oldest one registered in Texas. He knew that the use of brands would prevent fights over ownership of livestock.

He was a brave person. He fought to keep Indians from taking his animals. He stood up to Spanish government officials, even went to prison, to protect his land and his livestock.

Modern day ranchers can understand the problems that Juan faced. Texas ranchers still brand their livestock. They also make sure they have clear titles to their land, livestock, and water.

Henry Jones

Republic of Texas Rancher

*WOULD YOU like to drive Texas cattle to
market in New Orleans?*
*Henry Jones would help you find a good
horse for the 400-mile trip.*

We remember Henry Jones because he was a
rancher during the time of the Republic of Texas.
Four generations of his family have preserved the
Texas ranch he started in 1823.

His ranch now is known as the George Ranch
Historical Park. It was named after Mamie and
Albert George. Mamie was a descendant of Henry
Jones and his wife, Nancy.

George Ranch is located eight miles south of
Richmond, on the Brazos River. It was on this and
nearby ranches that Anglo-Texans and Afro-Texans
first ranched.

Henry Jones came to Texas from the state of Virginia. He and Nancy were among the first 300 settlers in Stephen F. Austin's Colony.

Henry Jones
— Courtesy George Ranch Historical Park,
Richmond, Texas

The George Ranch, 1996.
— Courtesy George Ranch Historical Park,
Richmond, Texas

When the Joneses arrived, Texas was a part of Mexico. Life was very hard in early Texas. Few people lived in Texas except Indians, who roamed the country. The only way to get other people to settle in Texas was to give them free land.

Henry and Nancy camped in Independence, Texas, to wait for their land grant to be handed out. Their first son, William, was born in their camp under a live oak tree. He was the first child born in Austin's Colony.

Henry was thirty-five years old when he received 4,428 acres of land. He moved his family into a simple cabin he built on their land. Soon another son, James, was born.

Usually, Indians were not a problem to settlers in Austin's Colony. One day, however, Henry faced an Indian problem. He had been away from home to get a supply of salt. When he got home, he was surprised to find his yard full of Indians.

They had not harmed Nancy or their sons. Still, Henry didn't know why the Indians had come. Then the Indians extended their hands in friendship. They were able to make Henry understand that they had won a battle against the Karankawa Indians. They wanted beef to eat during a celebration of their victory.

Henry gave them the meat. They feasted and danced there on his place for several days. He had to kill more animals for their feast before they finally had celebrated enough. Then they mounted their ponies and rode away.

The first Jones daughter, Mary Moore Jones, nicknamed Polly, was born in 1826. She grew up to be the one who preserved the history of her family.

The Joneses had plenty of food at their Texas home. Besides raising good gardens, they had beef, pork, chickens, and all kinds of wild game. Texans especially liked to eat buffalo, deer, and bear meat. Sometimes they also ate squirrel and opossum.

Henry set about developing the rich farm land on the River Place. Like some of his neighbors, Henry owned slaves. They cleared trees and brush from the Jones land and planted the crops. Henry knew that fields of corn and cotton would grow well in the warm, damp climate.

The nearby Brazos River was important to the Joneses. Sometimes Henry traveled by boat on business trips along the river. Before long, he built a wharf and a boat landing on the Brazos. He also built a ferry to carry people and goods across the river.

The family enjoyed watching the steamboat named *Yellowstone* pass by on the river. The boat ran on steam power made by burning wood. The boat captain sometimes stopped to buy wood from Henry.

When he first settled on his place, Henry spent most of his time farming. But he really wanted to be a stock raiser. He started a herd of beef cattle on the "stock farm," up on the prairie, away from the river.

Soon Nancy and the children also moved to their prairie place.

Henry used his initials for his brand. He recorded the brand at San Felipe, the seat of Texas government. Branding was sometimes the only way to identify his animals. He often sent a cowhand riding along his property line to keep the livestock from drifting away. No one had fences then.

The beef herd multiplied quickly and made Henry a prosperous cattle rancher. Then he added Longhorns that ran wild on the Texas prairie. He also tamed some small Spanish horses that wandered near his place.

Henry wanted even more cattle. He could sell or trade cattle to new settlers moving to Texas. The settlers wanted beef for food, of course. Pioneer women salted, smoked, or dried beef so that it would not spoil.

Beef had other uses. Candles were made of beef tallow. Horns could be carved into powder horns, horn spoons, or horn cups. Cow hides were good for making rawhide furniture seats, bed ropes, or laces for tying.

Not many people had money to buy cattle at a price of $25 each. Instead, they would work for Henry long enough to pay for the animals they wanted.

Nancy's dog-trot prairie home now is the site of the George Ranch House. A log kitchen and a log dining room stood behind the house. Nearby was a cow pen for milk cows, a horse pen, and a log barn that held livestock feed. Further away was a collecting pen, used during cattle roundups.

Nancy was always very busy at home with her large family to care for. She hired teachers to live in the home and instruct the children when they were school age. The home was a convenient place for travelers to stop. Also, it was used as a place to vote in Austin's Colony.

In 1836, the Texas Revolution developed. The Texans declared their independence from Mexico. In the war that followed, General Santa Anna and his Mexican troops captured the Alamo in San Antonio.

Henry joined the Texas army but was sent home to help his family. The Joneses and other Texas settlers fled toward East Texas ahead of the Mexican army. Their flight became known as the "Runaway Scrape."

As it turned out, Henry was too ill to ride his horse on their flight. He rode in a wagon that could be driven aboard the Jones ferry to cross the Brazos River. That meant Nancy had a sick husband, a newborn daughter, and six other children to worry over during the terrible trip. Polly, age nine, and her two older brothers did all they could to help their mother.

The Texans won the battle at the San Jacinto Battle Ground. Texas became an independent country, the Republic of Texas. It then was safe for the Jones family to return home.

Henry became a very wealthy man during the years of the Republic. By 1840, he was the seventh largest stock raiser in Texas. Every spring he organized "cow hunts" or roundups to brand livestock. The fall roundups helped him gather cattle to drive to market in New Orleans. At that city, Jones could trade his cattle for cash or for manufactured goods.

Young Polly Jones married William M. Ryon in 1845. Her parents invited all their neighbors to a fine wedding and to the feast that followed. Henry had pits dug, over which mutton, veal and pork were barbecued. A long table held every good food available. Known for his fiddle-playing, Henry kept the wedding guests dancing well into the night. Polly and William Ryon settled on their property near her parents and raised three children there.

About this time, Henry and Nancy decided to replace the log cabin on the prairie. They built a two-story plantation home. Sam Houston was one of many visitors to the home.

Nancy died in 1851 at age forty-seven, and Henry died ten years later. They are buried in the family cemetery on the old place. Their property was the second most valuable in Fort Bend County at that time. It was worth more than $200,000, with over 7,000 cattle.

Polly Jones Ryon represented the next generation left to carry on traditions started by Henry and Nancy. Polly and her husband bought the old home on the prairie from family members in 1869.

The Ryons ran the ranch until William's death in 1875. Polly then registered her own brand and continued ranching. She was one of the first ranchers in the area to begin using barbed wire fences. That meant her cattle no longer grazed on open range.

When Polly died in 1896, she willed her property to her three children. The old home, however, went to her granddaughter Mary (Mamie) Davis. Polly asked Mamie to keep the place in the family as long as possible.

Mamie Davis married Albert George the same year Polly died. The discovery of oil on the ranch property in the 1920s helped Mamie and Albert George financially. After the old home burned down, they built another house on the same site. It is preserved at the George Ranch Historical Park.

Mamie and Albert George had no children to inherit the ranch. They chose to give it to the people of Fort Bend County. Land and funds went to the

George Foundation to preserve old family homes and to build the George Ranch Historical Park.

Mamie also donated family documents, photographs, clothing, and furniture. These items, along with the stories of Henry Jones and family members who inherited the prairie land, are part of the ranch museum.

Richard King

King of the King Ranch

*COULD YOU protect cattle from bandits on
the Wild Horse Desert?
Richard King would have hired you.*

As a young man, Richard King came from New York
to Texas. He worked as a riverboat pilot for his
friend Captain Mifflin Kenedy. The two men came to
Texas to make money with the riverboat along the
Rio Grande. Then Richard used his money to begin
cattle ranching. He started his famous ranch in
1853. With help from his friend Kenedy, Richard
bought a 75,000-acre tract between Corpus Christi
and Brownsville. The ranch was one of the first large
Anglo-owned ranches in the dangerous area called
the Wild Horse Desert. It also was known as the
Nueces Strip. Richard stocked the place with as
many wild mustangs and Longhorns as his men
could round up.

The year after he bought his first land, Richard

Captain Richard King of the famous King Ranch.
— Courtesy King Ranch Archives

married Henrietta Chamberlain. He had met her during his riverboat days. She was the daughter of a missionary in Brownsville. She learned all she could about ranch life before she moved to ranch headquarters.

Henrietta turned a lonely outpost into a home for her family. She raised the five King children at the ranch house on Santa Gertrudis Creek.

Richard was not a tall man, but he was tough. He could hold his own in a fight to defend his property from outlaws. He built a stockade and blockhouse at ranch headquarters. Then he hired cowboys who knew how to use rifles to help him guard the place.

Most of the men who worked for Richard were Mexican *vaqueros*. They and Richard learned from each other. The *vaqueros* had great skill in handling livestock. They had learned everything from their fathers, who had worked on Spanish and Mexican ranches.

Richard had different skills. From his riverboat background, he could add ideas and technology. For him, the ranch was more than just a place to live. He also wanted it to become a business that would make money.

He added more land and more livestock whenever he could. Then, he began to think of ways to make his property better. To get water for cattle, he began by building dams across dry creeks. The dams would hold any rain water that might fall.

Richard always tried to find a market that would pay a good price for his livestock. At first, he sold cattle to buyers from Mexico. Later, he drove cattle or shipped them by boat to market in New Orleans.

47

He decided, also, to have better livestock. He bought Shorthorn cattle from Kentucky to mix with his best Longhorns. But he had a problem. Texas had no fences to keep his good stock away from the wild cattle.

Barbed wire for fences had not been invented then. The only thing Richard knew to do was to have his men build wooden fences all the way around the King Ranch. The fences were very expensive. Soon, however, other ranchers began to fence their land too. Richard and Captain Kenedy had helped bring an end to the open range in Texas.

Meanwhile, Richard still owned some riverboats. They made a good profit for him during the Civil War in the 1860s. That income meant he could afford to pay for new cattle and more fencing materials.

After the Civil War, in 1867, Richard began marking his cattle with the Running W brand. No one knows for sure why he chose the brand. But it became one of the best known brands in ranching.

Richard decided he could make more money by sending cattle herds up the trail to Kansas. There, trains would pick them up and take them on to markets. Through the years, more than 100,000 head of King Ranch cattle headed north to market to feed a beef-hungry nation.

Workers on the ranch always had trouble finding enough water for livestock. Then a new invention, the windmill, brought help for ranchers in the 1870s. They used wind power to pump water from hand-dug wells on the ranches.

Richard became ill and died in 1885. At the time, he held title to 500,000 acres of land. More than 80,000 head of cattle wore the Running W brand.

He left the ranch and livestock to his wife, Henrietta. She had lived on the ranch for thirty years. She knew how hard her husband had worked to build their King Ranch empire.

The family lawyer, Robert J. Kleberg, helped Henrietta King manage the ranch. Later, Robert married the Kings' daughter, Alice.

Robert soon became well known in ranching circles. He followed Richard King's plans for the ranch and brought in good livestock, including fine horses from Kentucky.

He helped nearby Corpus Christi become an important seaport. With advice from Henrietta, Robert donated land for the founding of "her town," Kingsville. Mrs. King helped it to become a place of churches, good schools, and good neighbors. In later years, a university was built at Kingsville.

Robert built railroads across the ranch to pick up cattle and take them to market. A town grew up where King Ranch cattle were loaded on the trains. The settlement was named "Alice," in honor of Robert's wife.

He had many problems to solve on the ranch. When Texas cattle died of a strange disease, Robert asked scientists to find out why they died. They learned that cattle ticks caused the disease. Then, Texas passed a law to get rid of the ticks. For several years, the law required all stockmen in the state to dip their cattle.

On the King Ranch, Robert designed the first

dipping vat. It was a pit dug in the ground and lined with concrete. The vat held water with enough arsenic to kill ticks. Livestock were forced to swim through the vat.

With more livestock on the ranch every year, Robert needed to find more drinking water for them. He began looking for a way to drill better wells for the windmills. After years of trying to find water, drillers brought in the first artesian well. Later, many more good wells were drilled to water King Ranch livestock.

Henrietta King died in 1925. By then, she had seen her son-in-law, Robert Kleberg, Sr., expand the King Ranch to include a million acres.

Robert continued his work at the ranch for forty-seven years. He added another 250,000 acres before his death in 1932. He had built up ranch livestock to more than 94,000 head of cattle and 4,500 horses and mules. He was very proud to have brought better livestock and better water sources to the ranch.

After 1935, the ranch land and investments were divided among all King heirs. Alice King Kleberg and her two sons and three daughters kept the Santa Gertrudis headquarters and the present King Ranch.

Many changes came to the ranch after Richard King's time. More than 2,000 miles of net wire replaced lumber fences around the property. Also, the ranch began to have as much income from oil and gas wells as from livestock. Hunters added more to ranch income.

Four-wheel-drive pickups came into ranch use about 1920. Pickups and trailers, along with good roads, changed ranch work. Cowboys then drove pickups more than they rode horses.

Longhorns disappeared from the King Ranch before the 1930s. Then the ranch made history with the development of a new breed of cattle. The Santa Gertrudis breed, deep red in color, was a mixture of Shorthorn, Hereford, and Brahman cattle.

The King Ranch sprawled across 825,000 acres of South Texas. It was larger than the entire state of Rhode Island. The ranch stocked more than 60,000 Santa Gertrudis cattle and 1,000 registered quarter horses.

The story of the King Ranch really is the story of Richard King's work and his dream of building a Texas ranch. Most of the owners of King Ranch property today are his descendants. Many employees on the ranch are descendants of the original King Ranch *vaqueros* who came to work for Richard King.

Charles Goodnight
— Courtesy Panhandle-Plains
Historical Museum

Charles Goodnight

Trailblazer and Ultimate Cowboy

WOULD YOU like to hunt buffalo with Comanche Chief Quanah Parker? Charles Goodnight was his friend.

Charles Goodnight became a famous rancher the hard way. He had nothing to begin with but his own intelligence and hard work. He built large cattle herds that brought him fame.

Charles was ten years old when he moved with his family from Illinois to East Texas in 1836. The boy didn't have much time to go to school. But before he reached Texas, he had learned to read and write.

He found lots more things to learn in Texas. As their wagon train reached Texas, Charles saw buffalo for the first time. Then, when the family settled in Milam County, he learned how to build a log house.

At age nineteen, Charles and his stepbrother Wesley were ready for an adventure. They used all their money to buy a heavy wagon. Then they bought three saddle horses and a team of oxen to pull the wagon. The plan was to reach the gold fields of California to get rich.

After weeks of travel west, they still hadn't made it across Texas. The state was too large. They were so disappointed that they decided not to go to California. Instead, they drove the wagon toward Waco.

At the Brazos River, they met a man named Varner, who needed help with his cattle. Varner liked the herding skills the young men had. He offered them a nine-year contract to handle his cattle business. He promised to give them one-fourth of the calf crop each year as their pay.

The young men took the job. Things went so well that, in a few years, they had their own herd of 4,000 cattle. They took the cattle to Palo Pinto County, west of Fort Worth. They knew that Indians would be a problem there. But the grass would be better for cattle.

The Civil War started in 1861. Instead of joining the army, Charles chose to become a scout for the Texas Rangers. While other men went to war, the Rangers had to protect the men's homes and families from Indian raiders.

Charles always remembered one of his Ranger experiences in North Texas. On that day, he was riding with Ranger Captain Sul Ross. They attacked and defeated some Comanche Indians. Among the captives was a woman. She was weeping because her husband, Chief Nocona, died in the battle.

Charles told the captain, "She's a white woman. Indians don't have blue eyes like hers."

The woman was identified as Cynthia Ann

Parker. The Indians had captured her when she was a little girl in East Texas. They had spared her life. When she grew up, she married Nocona. She had lived as a Comanche for twenty-five years.

When Captain Ross contacted Cynthia Ann's family in East Texas, her uncle came to take her home. Charles heard later that she was not able to adjust to living with her white relatives. She soon died in East Texas.

Cynthia Ann was survived by her Indian son Quanah, a Comanche chief. Years later, Charles would get to meet Quanah.

While Charles was away working with the Rangers, he lost most of his cattle. Some of them strayed away, and thieves stole some. When the war was over, he had to start over to build up a herd.

In 1866, Charles met another cattleman, Oliver Loving. The two became fast friends. They decided to open a trail-driving business, a new adventure for them. Eighteen cowboys helped them make up a herd of 2,000 Longhorn cattle in Palo Pinto County.

For their first trail drive, they wanted to take along a new invention the cowboys were talking about. The new invention was fastened to the rear end of a heavy wagon. It was a chuck box to hold food and cooking vessels. A door was hinged at the bottom and latched at the top. The door had a swinging leg. When the door was set down, the leg rested on the ground. The door became a food table. The cook thought this "chuck wagon" would make his work easier.

Most trail drives headed north toward Kansas. But Charles wanted to try something different. He and Oliver decided to head the cattle 600 miles westward toward Fort Sumter in New Mexico. The partners had to blaze their own trail, the Goodnight-Loving Trail, across the plains. Comanche and Apache Indians were constant threats. But the worst part of the trip was getting across the nintey-six miles of desert.

They couldn't stop to rest or sleep at all. They had to keep the cattle moving to get them to the Pecos River before they died of thirst. The cook set up his chuck wagon ahead of the cattle. Then the men would eat and drink whenever they drove the cattle past the wagon.

For Charles and Oliver, their first drive was a great success. They made it across the desert without any loss of livestock. When they got the cattle to New Mexico, .they sold at a good price, eight cents a pound. That gave them enough gold and silver coins to pay off the cowboys.

The next problem was getting their own $6,000 in coins back to Texas to buy a new herd. They loaded the money and food for the eighteen cowboys on a pack mule and started home. In a night camp on the way back, the mule became frightened by a wolf's howl. The animal galloped away across the plains.

Charles finally caught the mule and saved the money. The food supplies were lost, scattered for miles. The men had nothing to eat until a kind wagon master gave them food near the Pecos River.

Charles and Oliver led another drive together. Then Indians killed Oliver Loving on the third drive. Charles was very sad after the loss of his friend. But he continued the drives to New Mexico and Colorado for three years.

Charles always relied on a lead steer named "Old Blue" to help with the herds. The steer wore a brass bell around his neck. The men and the cattle could hear that bell and try to keep the pace set by Old Blue.

The steer went up the trail for eight years, sometimes twice a year. He had a way of calmly leading cattle through a situation that might frighten them. That way, he kept them from stampeding. He would bravely plunge into river crossings and get the cattle to follow him quickly. He seemed to know that he was the boss of the cattle.

At the end of a cattle drive, the cowboys had to get their lead steer and the saddle horses back home to start the next drive. On one return trip, Kiowa Indians decided they wanted to eat Old Blue for dinner. The cowboys had to work fast to defend their old friend. Finally, Old Blue retired to grassland and lived to the age of twenty.

Then Charles married a schoolteacher named Mary Ann Dyer. He decided to quit the dangerous life on the trail.

He remembered that he had seen a very large canyon in the Texas Panhandle. He thought that canyon would be a good place to raise cattle. Steep cliffs would protect the animals from bad weather and predators. Within those canyon walls, Charles would not need to build fences to hold the stock. The canyon was sixty miles long, 1,000 feet deep, and as much as fifteen miles wide in some places. It had water, grass, and trees.

Centuries before, Indians had named the area Palo Duro, or "hard wood." They made arrows from the canyon's strong cedar brush.

Charles and Mary Ann hired a few men to drive the cattle to the Palo Duro. After a long, hard journey, they arrived at the great canyon. Still more work lay ahead. The rocky slopes were too rough and too steep. Their wagons could not follow the cattle down into the canyon. Charles and his men had to use ropes to let the wagons and supplies down to the floor of the canyon.

Charles was willing to do all the work necessary to build a ranch. But he needed money to buy more ranch land. The following year, he formed a partnership with John Adair, an investor from Ireland.

John Adair's money bought 12,000 acres of Palo Duro Canyon, at a price of $1 per acre. The ranch took its name and the JA brand from the initials of John Adair.

Charles then began one of the greatest ranches and cattle empires of the Texas Panhandle.

When the railroad came through their settlement, a town was established and called Goodnight. Mary Ann helped develop schools and churches in the area.

Charles and Mary Ann lived sometimes as much as 100 miles from their nearest neighbor. In spite of that, they attracted many visitors to their home. They had no children, but Mary Ann helped look after the cowboys as if they were family. She patched clothes, cooked favorite foods, and doctored sick cowboys.

Charles was mild-mannered and kindly. He would not employ cowboys who were trouble makers. He wanted them to take good care of their horses and wash their saddle blankets once a week. Any cowboy who raked his horse with spurs was fired on the spot.

In early history, the canyon was range land for the American bison or buffalo. When Charles moved to the Palo Duro, he constantly saw men killing buffalo. Most of the animals had been destroyed by 1885.

Charles and other ranchers started working to keep the buffalo from becoming extinct. He began in a small way, by bringing home any stray buffalo calf he found. As years passed, he developed his own herd of buffalo.

For years, Charles was a close friend of Kiowa, Comanche, and Taos Indians. He listened to their lore and learned about their culture. He was finally given the chance to meet Quanah Parker, the Comanche chief and son of Cynthia Ann Parker, in 1878.

Quanah and his tribe had been sent to live on a reservation at Fort Sill, Oklahoma. One day, however, he appeared in the canyon with many braves and squaws. They wanted to hunt buffalo just once more, as they had done in the old days.

Charles provided them two beeves a day. The group stayed for several weeks. Then they returned to Fort Sill.

Charles had many friends in ranching. In 1880 he helped organize the Panhandle Stockmen's Association. The members worked together to improve their cattle. They also tried to rid the area of outlaws and cattle thieves.

Through the years, Charles continued to buy more land and more cattle for the JA Ranch. Eventually the ranch had 100,000 cattle grazing on 1,325,000 acres of land. After twelve years, Charles sold out his interest and moved to the town of Goodnight. He took his buffalo with him wherever he lived. He built up one of the largest buffalo herds in the world.

The buffalo made the Goodnight ranch famous. He could sell them for fancy prices. Once in a while, he staged an old-fashioned buffalo hunt. His Indian friends did the hunting, and hundreds of other people came to see the event.

Charles Goodnight died at age ninety-one. He is remembered as a conservationist, trailblazer, and Texas Ranger. On the JA Ranch, he built one of the greatest cattle empires in Texas. Most of all, he is remembered as an excellent cowboy.

The Cowboy Hall of Fame opened in Oklahoma City years later. The name of Charles Goodnight was the first to be honored there.

George W. Saunders

The Trail Driver Who Wrote All About It

WOULD YOU believe a cowboy ghost story? George W. Saunders collected all kinds of cowboy stories.

Rancher George Washington Saunders was born in Gonzales County in 1854. Everyone knew that George's father liked to name his sons after American presidents.

Most of his family members worked with livestock all their lives. They had moved their herd of cattle from Mississippi to Texas after George was born. They liked to say that George went on his first cattle drive when he was five years old. That was when they moved down the road to Goliad County. George rode a horse using his sister's side saddle and brought up the tail end of the cattle herd.

Cattle often strayed from their home range because Texas didn't have fences then. Every year, settlers living within about thirty miles of the Saunders

George W. Saunders, the rancher who collected stories.
— Courtesy Texas Pioneers Trail
Drivers Texas Rangers Museum

place would meet for a "cow hunt," to round up stray stock.

Usually a cow hunt lasted about two weeks, until all cattle were gathered and held in herd. Then each owner took his own cattle home. He branded some and sold others. Owners would range-herd their own cattle until time for the next cow hunt. If cattle were not rounded up or herded, they became too wild.

Things went well for George's family until the Civil War started. Soon afterward, older members of the family left for the Confederate Army.

When George was ten, he and his brother Jack were the only boys left to take care of the livestock until the war was over. The mustang horses that ran wild in Texas caused the brothers lots of trouble. They had to keep the mustangs away or else the family's horses would become wild too.

A really good thing happened to George when he was ten years old. That was the year he chose the brand he used for the rest of his life. It was a half-circle above the number 10. He called it the "Half-Circle Ten" brand.

After the war, Texans had many more cattle than they needed. Texans began taking cattle on trail drives toward Kansas. At the end of the trail, cattle were loaded on railroad cars and sent to Chicago cattle buyers. The original cattle owners paid men who worked on the drives.

George made his first real trail drive in 1870,

when he was barely seventeen years old. Jim Byler was "trail boss." They started north from Stockdale with 1,000 steers, headed for Abilene, Kansas.

Things went well as they passed through Gonzales, Lockhart, Austin, and Georgetown.

Then, on the river near Georgetown, a thunderstorm caused a bad stampede. The herd was split into several bunches. All were found the next day except seventy-five steers. Young George Saunders also was missing. The boss finally found George and the steers, together, ten miles down the river.

George expected the boss to be angry with him. But he explained that he couldn't find the trail. He didn't know what direction to go to find the herd.

Jim didn't fuss at George. He liked the boy's answer well enough. At least George had kept the seventy-five steers together.

They traveled on northward through Waco and Fort Worth and crossed the Red River. George learned how to make the cattle swim across many rivers along the way.

They took the Chisholm Trail on through Indian Territory, now called Oklahoma. George saw buffalo for the first time just before they reached Kansas in May. They stopped their herd near Abilene, Kansas, where a cattle buyer met them.

After all the cattle were sold, George traveled back home to Texas with fifty other cowboys. Along with them were five chuck wagons, five cooks, and about 150 horses.

At one river, they had trouble crossing. The flooding river was very swift and deep. The cowboys built a raft of logs. Then, they had to have a rope stretched across the river to keep the raft from washing down the river. Four of the cowboys tried to swim across with the end of the rope. Each cowboy failed. George was the fifth one to try. He was determined to make it.

George took one end of the rope in his mouth and swam out into the water. He got so tired, fighting the swift water. Finally, he made it across. He heard happy cowboy yells when he climbed out of the water and tied the end of the rope to a tree.

Every spring for several years, George went up the trail with herds. He often saw Indians during those drives. Once, while George was on the Comanche Indian Reservation, the Comanches demanded horses and supplies. Both George and the old chief could speak Spanish. They were the ones who did the talking. George agreed to give them one horse and some supplies. This seemed to please the Indians.

Later, the Indians helped the cowboys. When the Texans had started moving their cattle again, twenty young Indian braves on beautiful horses came to ride with them. They helped swim the horses across the Canadian River. When several Texas horses bogged in the quicksand, the Indians helped rescue the horses. When the work was finished, the Indians showed off their riding skills to entertain the cowboys.

The first pasture fences were built in Texas about 1873. Fences helped ranchers keep up with their livestock. But fences brought other problems when some people began to cut them down. Ranchers started sending cowboys to ride along the fence line. The line riders watched to be sure no one was cutting fences and rustling cattle.

George's sister, Mary Saunders Henry, used to tell him a story about a ghostly line rider. The ghost appeared to a *vaquero* named Juan many years ago.

Juan had ridden his horse to see about some cattle. When a heavy rain suddenly started, he found a dry place in a deserted schoolhouse. It stood next to a graveyard. The storm brought darkness. Juan tried not to notice the lightning that flashed across the old gravestones outside the school.

He hoped that morning would come quickly and stop the storm. Instead, in the morning the sky was still cloudy and dark. Heavy rainfall continued. Juan stayed in the schoolhouse so long that he used the last of his jerky and coffee.

Suddenly, he could see the figure of a rider outside the building. The shadowy horseman trailed along the fence. He wore a black hat that covered much of his face. The man always stared down at the fence as he rode.

When the man rode nearer, Juan called to him. He was close enough to have heard Juan. But he rode on, never looking up. The man was riding line and seemed not to want to stop to talk.

At first, Juan was angry when the man did not even speak. Then Juan had other thoughts. He realized that the rider had made no sound. The dark figure passed along the fence and down the hill, but made no sound.

An hour later, the man in black rode back along the fence again. He still rode slowly and silently. He still watched the fence line, never looking elsewhere.

Then, as Juan watched, the rider turned from the fence. He passed by the graveyard and disappeared. Juan thought about following him. But then the rain stopped. It seemed more important for Juan to get out of that place.

Back at the ranch house, Juan went to find the foreman. He asked the foreman what kind of crazy man he had hired to ride fence.

The foreman listened carefully to Juan. He asked Juan for more details. Then the foreman and the other hands hurriedly got on their horses and rode toward the old cemetery.

After several hours, the men came back. They brought with them three rustlers. They told about finding more than a hundred head of cattle that the outlaws had stolen.

The foreman tried to explain everything to Juan. "Yes, you saw our fence rider," he said. "But he's dead now. Ten years ago, some rustlers shot him. He's buried in that little cemetery. If someone cuts our fences, his ghost rides the line. He rides until he finds where the fence is down. Then he goes back to his hillside. I asked you which direction he rode and how long he was gone. From what you told me, we knew where to find the rustlers."

George heard lots of cowboy stories while he was making the cattle drives. He also learned a lot about buying and selling livestock. That was why, after fifteen years of trail drives, he could tell that the drives were no longer getting good prices for cattle.

He decided to look for another kind of livestock market. In 1886 his company was named the George W. Saunders Live Stock Commission Company. The company really helped South Texas ranchers. It meant that they didn't have to send the cattle up a long trail to market. Instead, they could take their livestock to San Antonio to sell them.

George invited livestock buyers to come to his barns. These buyers purchased the livestock that ranchers had left there. Each rancher paid George a small fee for arranging the sale.

George also had an office near the railroad depot. Then he could ship cattle by train from San Antonio to other markets.

George also had a special interest in stock shows of all kinds. Sometimes he showed his own cattle. Other times he rode his horse in a show to attract buyers and get higher prices for the livestock.

At a San Antonio fair in 1892, he organized the first roping contest in the country. It was a good way for horsemen to show off their skills and the abilities of their horses. Since that time, public roping contests have been a popular feature of rodeos.

In his later years, George thought of a way to honor old trail drivers. He organized the Trail Drivers Association in San Antonio and served as the first president of the group.

The colorful old trail drivers were happy to join the organization. They liked George W. Saunders and liked to get together and retell the old stories.

George thought that cattle drives were an important chapter in the history of Texas cattlemen. He wanted to get their stories written down for others to read.

The problem was that writing was hard for the old cowboys. Most of them had not gone to school very many years. But, in 1925, George had collected enough photographs and stories to fill two books. He called the volumes *Trail Drivers of Texas*.

George W. Saunders died July 3, 1933. The Pioneer Trail Drivers Museum in San Antonio honored him. Also, his name was listed in the South Texas Cowboy Hall of Fame during the Cowboy Homecoming in Pleasanton in 1970.

Charles Schreiner of Kerrville.
—Courtesy of Charles Schreiner III

Charles Schreiner

Businessman/Rancher of the Y O

WHERE WOULD you work if you had no money?

Charles Schreiner could always help you find a job.

Charles Schreiner was only fourteen when he and his family arrived in San Antonio from France in 1852. He had to work instead of going to school. He educated himself through his work.

At age sixteen, he enlisted in the Texas Rangers. It was the only way he could earn a man's wages. In the hard work as a Ranger, he got to see a lot of Texas country.

After two years, he left the Rangers and bought a ranch he had found on Turtle Creek in Kerr County. He built a log cabin by hand and took his new wife, Lena, to live there in October 1861.

Then, for three years, he had to be away from home, serving in the Confederate Army during the Civil War. After the war was finally over, he returned to San Antonio by train. There he asked about the cost of a ride to Kerrville. When he heard the price, he shook his head. He had only five gold dollars of army pay in his pocket.

To save his money, he walked the seventy-five miles back to his cabin. His wife was waiting with their young son, Aime Charles.

The years from 1865 to 1869 were very hard years for the Schreiners. Like other Texans after the war, Charles ran out of money. Bad weather ruined his crops. He had to protect the livestock from coyotes, bobcats, and foxes. He knew that an Indian raid could come any time.

After four years of ranch work, Charles was elected to county office in Kerrville. Charles never said he was tired of ranching. It was just that he needed the salary that the office paid. Charles looked for other ways of making money. He could see that ranchers in the area needed a general store for supplies. With help from a partner, he opened the Schreiner store on Christmas Eve, 1869. He had to build a picket fence around the store to keep out stray animals. The fence was a good place to hitch horses while their owners traded for goods in the store.

By that time, outlaws were more of a problem than Indians. A company of "Minute Men" in Kerrville, with Charles as captain, guarded against such lawbreakers. When some horse thieves rode into Kerrville, Charles and his men killed one thief and chased the others out of the county. After that, Charles was called "Captain Schreiner."

From his store, Charles could watch the herds of Longhorn passing through town. Sometimes, the large, multicolored cattle strung out for hours at a time. They were on their way to market in Kansas.

Later he saw Texas cattlemen return from Kansas. They had money to spend in his store. It was the first time since the Civil War that Texans had money to spend.

Charles listened to the cowboys and the cattle owners. They told stories about their long trek north on the trail drives. From what Charles learned, he began to buy up more land and enough Longhorn cattle to get ready for a trail drive.

When it came time to make the first drive to Kansas, Charles had his cowboys put together a trail herd. Charles named a trail boss and picked out his lead steer. When eight cowboys and a camp cook were hired, the men pointed the Longhorns north.

Trail drives continued. By 1874, Charles and his partners had sent 150,000 cattle to Kansas markets.

On his ranch land, Charles looked for ways to improve his livestock. He added Hereford, Shorthorn, and Angus cattle. In 1880, he bought some cattle that came from Goliad County. The cattle already carried the Y O brand. To keep from rebranding

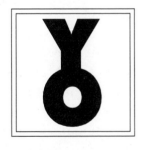

the cattle, he bought the brand also. He used it on his Longhorns, and it became an important part of Schreiner ranching history.

As years passed, Charles remained a storekeeper. In the store the cattlemen frequently paid Charles with Spanish gold coins worth $16. Charles kept an axe and chopping block handy. He cut off a piece of a coin and returned that piece to the customer for change.

His banking business developed because many cowmen gave Charles their excess cash for safe-keeping. He always gave them a receipt for their money. He kept his own money and his customers' money in a special box. Each night he put the box under his floor. He covered the opening in the floor with a barrel of salt. The store was robbed many times over the years. But no thief knew to look under the floor.

Charles became interested in sheep and Angora goats soon after he opened his store and bank. He soon saw that sheep and goat raisers had no way to get their wool and mohair to market.

He thought of a way to solve their problem and make money himself. At first ranchers stored their wool or mohair in his store. They paid Charles a fee when he found a market for them. He usually had to carry the goods to San Antonio by ox team to reach a market.

Later, he built warehouses to hold the wool and mohair in Kerrville. Then, in 1887, he got the San Antonio and Aransas Pass Railroad into town. The train tracks passed alongside Charles' warehouse on Schreiner Street so that the train could pick up wool and mohair. Ox teams no longer had to pull wagons to San Antonio. Charles' work to get markets for ranchers made Kerrville the mohair capital of the world.

Charles always wanted to help the ranchers and other people of the Kerrville area. He promoted the city water works, housing areas, a sawmill, and a cotton gin. He operated the first electric light and power plant. He also gave $42,000 for a highway leading from Rocksprings to Kerrville.

Oil resources were never found on his property to give him financial help. He had to find other ways to make money.

"Do what works" seemed to be his motto for making money. That motto caused him to raise any items that would bring in cash to his store, including pecans, eggs, and poultry.

By 1919 Charles owned well over half a million acres. In later years, Schreiner ranching was represented by the Y O Ranch, forty miles from Kerrville.

Charles bought the Y O Ranch in 1880. He left the 69,000-acre ranch to his son, Walter R. Schreiner. Later, Walter's son, Charles III, owned the Y O Ranch.

Like his grandfather, Charles III sought new ways to make the land pay. In 1957, he decided to buy some Longhorns. He knew they could adapt to the ranch.

Longhorns were almost extinct by then, however. They were hard to find. He finally bought some in Oklahoma. He helped get the Texas Longhorn Breeders Association started. In 1964, his small herd of Longhorns was the first to be registered.

Charles III decided to stage a trail drive. Longhorn steers would walk from Texas to Dodge City to get ranchers to notice the old cattle breed. He wanted the drive to be just like old times when his grandfather sent herds up the trail.

Longhorn owners in Texas and Oklahoma helped. Together, they rounded up nearly 100 head for the drive. That herd of Longhorns was large enough to make an impressive sight along the highways.

On June 26, 1966, the herd left San Antonio,

with 50,000 people watching. At the end of the 750-mile trail, the town of Dodge, Kansas, was ready to greet the trail drivers.

Thousands of people had seen their first Long-horns and a trail drive. The drive helped people understand that Longhorns are important to ranchers. After that, the Longhorn seemed to be safe from extinction.

Charles III then looked for other uses of the ranch land. He decided that hunting, tourism, game conservation, and outdoor education should be the major interests at the Y O.

He added exotic animals from foreign countries to the Y O collection. Visitors who entered the ranch gate knew to expect to see giraffes, zebras and ostriches, right along with the Longhorns.

An Outdoor Awareness Program was also started on the ranch. Young students attended programs in conservation, environmental education, and exotic wildlife.

The Y O Ranch went off in directions never dreamed of by the first Charles Schreiner. However, along with the new programs, the basics were still there: cattle, sheep, and goats. By making these changes, his descendants managed to hold on to the land and the old Y O brand.

The first Charles Schreiner is remembered as a rancher and a businessman who dealt fairly and honestly with others.

His name is stamped on the Kerrville area in ranching and in other ways. It lives on in the form of the Schreiner College, the Charles Schreiner Company store, the Charles Schreiner Bank, and the Schreiner Museum.

Places to Visit

Don't just sit there! Saddle up your horse (or fill up your tank) and get to these fascinating places in Texas...

... to learn about Spanish-Texans:
Institute of Texan Cultures, San Antonio
Goliad State Park (Mission Espiritu Santo), Goliad
Presidio La Bahia, Goliad
San Antonio Missions National Park, San Antonio

... to learn about citizens of the Republic of Texas:
The Alamo, San Antonio
The Cradle, Galveston
Daughters of the Republic of Texas Library,
    San Antonio
Daughters of the Republic of Texas Museum, Austin
French Legation, Austin
George Memorial Library, Richmond
Memorial Museum, Gonzales
San Jacinto Battleground, Houston
Star of the Republic Museum, Washington-on-the-
    Brazos

. . . to learn about ranching in Texas:

Alamo Village, Brackettville

George Ranch Historical Park, Richmond

King Ranch Museum, Kingsville

Longhorn Museum, Pleasanton

National Historic District, Fort Worth Stockyards, Fort Worth

Panhandle-Plains Historical Museum and Palo Duro State Park, Canyon

Pioneer Trail Drivers Museum, San Antonio

Ranching Heritage Center, Lubbock

Y O Ranch, Mountain Home

Milestones for
Famous Texas Ranchers

1762	Spanish-Texas rancher Juan Flores registered the first Texas cattle brand
1825	Henry Jones, Anglo-Texan, registered his brand at San Felipe, Texas.
1836-1846	The Republic of Texas was an independent nation.
1846-1848	United States and Mexico were at war over disputed land claims.
1852	Richard King started the King Ranch in the South Texas coastal country.
1861-1865	The Civil War was fought in the United States.
1866-1890	Ten million Texas cattle went north along cattle trails.
1870s	Windmills and barbed wire fencing were available for ranchers to use.
1876	Charles Goodnight founded the JA Ranch in Palo Duro Canyon.
1880	Kerr County rancher Charles Schreiner bought the YO brand and ranch.
1886	Rancher George W. Saunders opened a new market for Texas cattle.
1940	Watt Matthews became manager of the Lambshead Ranch near Albany.
1940s	Electricity was available on ranches in Texas.
1949	Farm-to-Market roads developed in Texas.

1959   John Wayne's movie *The Alamo* was filmed on Happy Shahan's Ranch.

1961   The problem of screwworms was solved.

1973-1979   Rancher Dolph Briscoe, Jr., served as governor of Texas.

1991   Rancher Mary Nan West became a regent of the Texas A&M University System.

Ranching Words

barrel racing — a rodeo event; horse riders race around large barrels set in a pattern.

bay — a reddish brown color.

blockhouse — a heavily reinforced building.

bootjack — a forked device to help pull a boot off.

brand — a mark made on the skin of livestock, using a hot iron, to show ownership.

brindled — grayish color with streaks or spots.

brood mare — a female horse kept for breeding.

browse — to feed on leaves or twigs of trees and brush.

castrate — to remove an animal's ability to reproduce.

chuck wagon — a mobile kitchen for serving food to ranch hands.

cull — to pick out or separate from a group.

dog-trot house — two rooms with a breezeway between, all under one roof.

drench — to give medication.

drought — no rain for a long time; drouth.

exotic wildlife — animals from foreign countries.

hacienda — Spanish word for a large house in the country.

heifer — a young cow.

inoculate — to give a shot of medicine to protect a person/animal from disease.

leasing — allowing someone to use or rent land that belongs to you.

leggings — a covering to protect a cowboy's legs.

line riders — those who ride up and down the fence line to check for breaks.

open range — no fences are used to mark property lines.

Old Three Hundred — the first families in Stephen F. Austin's colony in Texas.

presidio — Spanish word for town, village.

prickly pear — a type of cactus that has an edible fruit.

rustling — stealing cattle.

section of land — 640 acres.

screwworms — blowfly larvae that feed on living animals.

shearing — clipping wool from sheep or mohair from goats.

stallion — an adult male horse.

stockade — a fenced area to keep in cattle/horses.

suet — hard, fatty tissue of cattle or sheep, used in cooking or making tallow.

toe fenders — a part of the stirrup on a saddle that protects the toe of the boot.

tourism — providing events and places that visitors will pay to see.

vaqueros — Spanish word for cowboys or those who round up livestock.

volunteer — a person who works without pay.

wean — take away mother's milk from a young animal and provide other nutrition.

Bibliography

Books:

Barrett, Neal, Jr. *Long Days and Short Nights: A Century of Texas Ranching on the YO, 1880-1890.* Mountain Home, TX: YO Press, 1980.

Buck, Samuel M. *Yanaguana's Successors: The Story of the Canary Islanders' Immigration into Texas in the 18th Century.* Robert M. Benavides, 1980.

Clayton, Lawrence. *Historic Ranches of Texas.* Austin: University of Texas Press, 1993.

Clayton, Lawrence. *Watkins Reynolds Matthews: Biography of a Texas Rancher.* Austin: Eakin Press, 1994.

Douglas, C.L. *Cattle Kings of Texas.* Austin: State House Press, 1989.

Fehrenbach, T. R. *Lone Star: A History of Texas and the Texans.* New York: Macmillan, 1968.

Graham, Joe S. *El Rancho in South Texas: Continuity and Change from 1750.* Denton, TX: University of North Texas Press, 1994.

Hunter, John Marvin. *Trail Drivers of Texas.* Austin: University of Texas Press, 1985.

Jackson, Jack. *Los Mesteños: Spanish Ranching in Texas, 1721-1821.* College Station: Texas A&M University Press, 1986.

McCoy, Dorothy Abbott. *Texas Ranchmen.* Austin: Eakin Press, 1987.

Rogers, Mondel. *Old Ranches of the Texas Plains.* College Station: Texas A&M University Press, 1976.

Weddle, Robert S., and Robert H. Thonhoff. *Drama and Conflict.* Austin: Madrona Press, 1976.

Articles:

Bowlin, Michael. "'Happy' Shahan Lures Hollywood to Brackettville," *Texas Co-op Power*, November 1994.

Kelton, Elmer. "The Longhorn Lives," *Texas Highways*, July 1991.

"Legend of George Saunders," *Pleasanton Express*, August 26, 1970.

Miller, Lauraine. "Boss Lady," *Texas*, Houston Chronicle Magazine, August 7, 1994.

Moore, Michael R. "Jones Stock Farm Interpretive Master Plan," George Ranch Historical Park, 1994.

Schreiber, Colleen. "With Fingers Crossed, Daughter of Rancher Follows Dad's Lead," *Livestock Weekly*, April 29, 1993.

More Stories about Ranching

Alexander, Frances. *Orphans on the Guadalupe*. Austin: Eakin Press, 1971.

Dobie, J. Frank. *The Longhorns*. New York: Grosset and Dunlap, 1941.

Hoff, Carol. *Johnny Texas*. Dallas: Hendrik-Long Publishing Co., 1992.

Mauzey, Merritt. *Texas Ranch Boy*. New York: Abelard-Schuman, Inc., 1955.

Moss, Helen. *Life in a Log Cabin on the Texas Frontier*. Austin: Eakin Press, 1982.

O'Rear, Sybil J. *Charles Goodnight, Pioneer Cowman*. Austin: Eakin Press, 1990.

Shub, Elizabeth. *The White Stallion*. New York: Greenwillow Books, 1982.

Thonhoff, Robert H. *El Fuerte del Cibolo: Sentinel of the Bexar-La Bahia Ranches*. Austin: Eakin Press, 1992.